A Mobius Path

poems by

Jean Fineberg

Finishing Line Press
Georgetown, Kentucky

A Mobius Path

Copyright © 2022 by Jean Fineberg
ISBN 978-1-64662-772-1 First Edition
All rights reserved under International and Pan-American Copyright Conventions. No part of this book may be reproduced in any manner whatsoever without written permission from the publisher, except in the case of brief quotations embodied in critical articles and reviews.

ACKNOWLEDGMENTS

As Above So Below Journal: "Ode to My Ballpoint Pen"
Every Day Poems: "Slither and Me"
FLARE: The Flagler Review: "Mistress of Toilets"
High Shelf Press: "English in Freefall"
Jewish Literary Journal: "Yahrzeit"
Literary Yard: "Aunt Lilli's Farmhouse;" "He Shot Somebody on 5th Avenue;" "Rubies;" "The Old Dancer"
Modern Poets Magazine: "Applesauce;" "Imposter Syndrome;" "The Mirror Speaks;" "We Never Made It to London"
Newtown Literary: "Aunt Mitzi's Last Stand"
Parliament Literary Journal: "Hiding is a Dirty Job"
Quillkeepers Press: "The Accidental Parent"
Riza Press Journal: "Demensch"
Scarlet Leaf Review: "Openings and Closings;" "The Accidental Parent"
Shot Glass Journal: "The Cha Cha Walk"
Soliloquies Anthology: "Fish Lips"
The Fibonacci Review: "Ailurophile;" "Light Blue;" "Treeamble"
Unlost Journal: "Cool Reason with a Chaser of Tears"
Vita Brevis Journal and Anthology: "Demensch"

Publisher: Leah Huete de Maines
Editor: Christen Kincaid
Cover Art and Design: Nicole Roberts
Author Photo: Myleen Hollero

Order online: www.finishinglinepress.com
also available on amazon.com

Author inquiries and mail orders:
Finishing Line Press
PO Box 1626
Georgetown, Kentucky 40324
USA

Table of Contents

Aunt Lilli's Farmhouse 1

The Old Dancer 2

Treeamble 3

Fish Lips 4

He Shot Somebody on 5th Avenue 5

Mistress of Toilets 7

We Never Made it to London 8

Rubies 9

The Mirror Speaks 10

The Accidental Parent 12

Hiding is a Dirty Job 13

Aunt Mitzi's Last Stand 14

If You Die First 15

Grazie Leonardo Fibonacci 16

Imposter Syndrome 17

Ode to My Ballpoint Pen 18

Fibonacci Rides Again 19

Slither and Me 20

Demensch 21

The Cha Cha Walk 22

Applesauce 23

Openings and Closings 24

Yahrzeit 26

Blue and Red 27

Cool Reason with a Chaser of Tears 28

English in Freefall 29

A Mobius Path 31

Aunt Lilli's Farmhouse

At Aunt Lilli's farmhouse every August,
my sister and I, two city girls, drink sweet
unpasteurized milk and race our cruisers
down country roads.

We hear the swoosh of Lilli's brush as she paints
alien landscapes with surreal flowers and arching
trees. Sometimes the trees look more like skeletons,
and the flowers, like fire.

We gather leaves for jumping, chase squirrels, and lose ourselves
in the tall corn maze. Lilli transforms the attic into a magical
treehouse with two rickety cots and private windows for spying.

Tiny white translucent petals float through the ragged screens,
spreading like summer snow on the sagging wooden floor. The
sun's dying rays shoot in one window and out the other like a
golden bridge.

Lilli does not sweep, lest she disturb their diaspora.
Downstairs, the adults smoke cigars, sip homemade
wine and retell old family secrets.

We sneak halfway down the ladder and catch
hushed sentences full of words we don't understand—
miscarriage, embezzlement, philanderer, incest.

At summer's curtain, our parents say we're old enough
to know more about Lilli. Finally divorcing that lying,
cheating, pilfering, no-good cheapskate of a husband, Lilli
sold the house. We head back to the city, silent, more thoughtful,
more grown up.

The Old Dancer

In my mother's attic, where
she stitched glittery costumes
and choreographed our dance
to "Me and My Shadow,"
time is a magazine, days
are in long meter, and spring
is the only season.

Her supple leather ballet shoes
grimace, wrinkle and harden,
satin pink fading to ghostly gray.

Her catlike body remembers
how to move—orchestral,
her trunk the staff, her
limbs the notes, her fingers
the flourishes.

Maple syrup eyes, skin
of dry blue rivulets, knees
creaking like screen doors.
Rhythms chiseled in her
bones refuse to leave
gracefully.

She doesn't remember
who she is, but we still
do that dance.

Treeamble
A Fibonacci poem

Leaf,
hand
of a
tulip tree,
coasting side to side
like an orchestra conductor's
baton, swinging to coax the violins to sweeten,
marry the up bows and down bows, form a more perfect union,
establish harmony.
The leafing tree proposes to secure blessings of
liberty and tranquility,
welfare and justice
in woodlots
and groves
for
all.

Fish Lips

You were splayed across the sand,
    a plastic bag
    clinging to your mouth
    and one eye staring.

"How long have you been here?" I asked.
    "Since the Cambrian explosion,"
    you burbled, exhaling, despite
    the bottle cap lodged in your gill.

"No, I mean you, yourself,"
    I said to the eye.
    "Not the point,"
    spat Fish Lips.

"First there were the forks,
    then the straws (RIP my sister),
    then the clamshell packaging,
    so insulting to clams."

"You hominids,
    a mere six million years old,
    threaten forebears
    a hundred times your age."

All four nostrils flaring,
    you flopped around
    and flipped me
    a pectoral fin.

Annoyed at this unfortunate interruption
    of my otherwise perfect day,
    I stepped over you, as your
    caudal fin spanked my sorry ass.

He Shot Somebody on 5th Avenue

> *"I could stand in the middle of Fifth Avenue and shoot somebody and I wouldn't lose any voters."* —Donald Trump

He shot somebody
    on 5th Avenue.
    Mothers ran for shelter,
    others ran for help.

A Kent State photo was taken.

The shooter,
    sporting a stupid grin
    and a stupider combover,
    vaporized into gold dust.

He blew into his limo,
    and arrived back
    at the castle in time
    for the evening news.

"Man commits suicide
    on Fifth Avenue,"
    ran the chyron
    on Fox News.

Satisfied,
    the shooter tweeted
    thoughts and prayers,
    although he had neither

After a respectable day or two, all was forgotten.

When I read "1984,"
    I knew it could happen.
    Truth is a potato chip in a thin glass dome,
    guarded by mercenaries.

When the order comes
	to smash the dome,
	and it will,
		what will replace it?

Mistress of Toilets

Now that you're gone, I mark all the toilets
and commandeer all the closets.

I replace the beer with coffee ice cream
and transform the ashtrays into jewelry beds.

I put my feet up on your desk
and flush your cologne.

I don't tend your tomatoes, but
they still grow plump and sweet.

I unhide the vibrator I bought when you
stopped wanting sex, when you stopped

letting me smooth your hair,
when you stopped laughing.

You say it wasn't the bicycle woman
with the sinewy legs, blond, unlike me,

or the flirty vet who winked at you when
she stroked the cat with her graceful hands.

You say you were drowning, "engulfed
in my aura," whatever the hell that means.

Now I rule from my throne,
Mistress of Closets and Toilets.

We Never Made it to London

Sometimes, when the fog
descends like the credits
of a film noir movie,

I put on your black sweater,
your long black raincoat,
take your black umbrella,

and walk by the East River.
I pretend it's the Thames; the
Brooklyn Bridge is London Bridge.

I amble past the clocksmith
and gaze at broken cuckoo clocks,
pendulums hoping to swing again.

I peek into the pet store. If I see
a black kitten, I pretend she's
Midnight starting another life.

I stop in a café, order black tea
and a tart, write glum sonnets
and hope I don't run into your new wife.

Rubies

Glistening ruby beads
on three parallel chains
parade across her teenage arm.

Slim shafts of sunlight
penetrate cracks in drawn
blinds, nighttime at noon.

Her hand squeezes a light bulb
until it shatters. She drags the
shards across her pale wrist.

Crimson droplets bubble
and spill onto her lap,
staining her skirt.

One wet red string
for her absent mother.

One wet red string
for her real father.

One wet red string
for her trapped brothers.

She will not mask these chains
with sleeves.

She will not flaunt them
as a badge for pity.

The Mirror Speaks

Pink scars peek out
from your red
knit cap, purple
patches from your
blue overalls.

I see you,
downcast eyes
steeled, a shield
to disguise
wounds unhealed.

I feel you
on the edge,
wedged between
desperation
and aspiration.

I hear you
try to minimize,
excise
your violation
with negation.

I watch your
stature, refined,
your ragtag shadow
shuffling behind,
incognito.

I see you
as a seed, your need
mud-caked, scraped,
raked across
a field of weeds.

I sense your borrowed
calm, see the totem rune
in your fisted palm,
hear your mournful tune
and whispered psalm.

Only in anxious dreams
with blurred cognition,
pain uncaged, do you
grant yourself permission
to scream and rage.

The Accidental Parent

When your mother admitted she's
not a kid person, I took you because
you needed to root in good soil.

When I checked your backpack for drugs
and made you change that shirt,
you never said "You're not my mom."

When I found your weed,
you asked to run away. I said,
"no, that's not how we solve things."

When I tried to take your arm,
you slipped it out of the sleeve
and didn't let me hug you.

When the police delivered you
stoned and drunk and you hit me,
I never said "You're not my child."

When you ignored me at graduation,
I snuck photos. You called me
auntie, I called you daughter.

When I gave you your
own wheels, you rolled
back to your family.

 Last time you called,
you chirped, "Hi mom!"
and we both laughed.

Hiding Is a Dirty Job

My best friend's parents
banned her from my bat mitzvah
and took her to church.

After they died,
Their hidden documents
outed them as Jews.

My college had 27 sororities—
22 Christian, 5 Jewish,
none lesbian.

Nobody knew I was a lesbian.
I dated fraternity boys
and hung out with townie girls.

My father drove across town
to a golf club where
nobody knew he was a Jew.

His brother Abraham
became "Albert Christian"
to get a job in the sewer.

His overalls smelled
of shit and methane
and lived outside the garage.

No amount of scrubbing
could buy them
a ticket indoors.

Aunt Mitzi's Last Stand

Mean old aunt Mitzi
planted her grudges in pots
and watered them every day.

Three daughters
of her three brothers
meet to honor her last wish.

Crouching at pier's end
in a January squall
on the Long Island Sound,

they ceremoniously
extract the urn
from its velvet purse,

conjure up
false memories
of her largesse

and affect solemnity,
as they pour her ashes
into the water.

An unsettling gust
flings white flakes
back into their faces.

For the last time,
Aunt Mitzi gets
the last word.

If You Die First

If you die first I will not persevere
or sport a stiffened British upper lip,
adopt a sham impregnable veneer—
I think I'll just break down and let 'er rip.

Breathe sour air, eat bitter tasting food
and writhe inside the corset of my gut.
Cough dusty flakes and splintered shards of wood
and choke with every gasp and searing cut.

Avert my eyes from winter's lovers, blessed,
who drew the longest straw, the calmest sky.
Although this weight lay leaden on my chest,
I will not be so lucky as to die.

But live without the spark of hope I cherish,
which part of me will darken when you perish.

Grazie Leonardo Fibonacci

I

The
Fib
poem is
a form based
on the structure of
the Fibonacci sequence, known
as phi, the golden ratio or golden number.
The beauty of the spiral it produces is enough for
some to believe in God.
The petals and placement of seed pods in a flower,
the way tree branches form or split, snail
and nautilus shells, hurricanes, hawk flight patterns,
animal bodies, proportions of the human face and
the DNA molecule.
One plus one equals two, then one plus two equals
three—two, three, five, eight, etcetera.
It's a place where math
and poets
converge
to
romp.

II

I
miss
her form
in my bed,
her long soft black hair
and her mellifluous meow.

Imposter Syndrome

Beware the fiend you fear and yet embrace—
the tiny voice that hisses in your ear.
The one which even time cannot erase—
the one which second guesses your career.

The words you write are really not your own.
They've all been written many times before.
Your paintings and your melodies are clones.
What makes you think your pieces will endure?

Why spend another hour, another year,
to add your voice to those who met the beast?
Compelled to tell the world that you were here—
your muse invoked, Calliope unleashed.

If you believe you're born to do this work,
fulfill your destiny and do not shirk.

Ode to My Ballpoint Pen

You willingly accept my loving grip
by hand or mouth or perched behind an ear,
or pocketed with your convenient clip.
Why must you, though, so often disappear?

There have been many others, I'll admit—
a piece of chalk, a felt-tipped pen or pencil.
Though you and I are such a perfect fit,
I wish your spring were not so temperamental.

Your plastic skin, resistant to abuse,
an object d'art for such a lowly price.
Compliantly, you offer of your juice,
although it's leaked or stuttered once or twice.

I'll mourn you when your lifeblood starts to thin
but find my consolation with your twin.

Fibonacci Rides Again

I
Wizzer

With
Fib
poems we
paint portraits
perched on a pinpoint.
Spin the whirling mass of silver
like a child's dreidel,
slowing to
reveal
gem
stones.

II
The Garlic Ritual

Smash
to
slacken
smooth buds from
crisp pale parchment skin.
Undress the clove until naked.
Olfaction magic
weaving an
ancient
Greek
spell.

Slither and Me

"Slither" doesn't exactly slide
off the tongue, but that's what happens
when an eight-year-old names a cat.

We hide our ages, lest
expectations become
inevitability.

She plops down the stairs,
her primordial pouch flapping.
I hop up, everything flapping.

Her whiskers turn white against
her thick black coat. My hair,
grizzled, frizzy, feral.

Hers eyes shine like a dimmed
party bulb. My eyes, once dark
chocolate, are now milky.

We still play with our toys—
 hers mousy,
mine digital.

We refuse to age gracefully.
 We plan to go clawing,
kicking and hissing.

Demensch
> *Mensch*: German for human
> *Demensch*: to remove what makes us human

She sits tiny in her wheelchair,
her regal head held high.

Her nubilous eyes wander,
seeking a landing strip.

She forgets she was a dancer
but her muscles remember.

Her biography is written
in disappearing ink—black, gray,

gone. We think there's nobody
there, but she listens.

"What's demench?" she asks.
"When you forget," I offer.

"Are you my mom?" I flounder.
"Yes, you were my mom, now I'm your mom."

Demensch: A dream—
You try to call,
but the numbers disappear.

You head home on the wrong bus.
Lost, always lost.

The Cha Cha Walk

In her nursing home garden, my mother and I
shuffle 'round the Mobius path.

I pluck a velvet leaf from the Lamb's Ear
and smooth it on her cheek.

We sing Sinatra songs, the soundtrack of my youth—
"Don't Get Around Much Anymore."

Lyrics that once clung to her neurons as I did
to her breast, exhausted, release their grip.

We do the Cha Cha Walk—
One, Two, OneTwoThree,
One, Two, OneTwoThree.

"Mom, do you know who I am?"
"Yes," she says, "someone who loves me."

Applesauce

Yesterday I fed my mother applesauce.
She smiled but she did not eat. Today
she lies dying in my arms, frail as a fawn.

I want my young mother who
cradled me, braided my hair,
played four hands on the piano.

I want my young mother who
embarrassed me teaching square
dancing at my middle school.

I want her to come again to my
graduation and tell everyone I was
first in our family to go to college.

I want her to sit in the front row again
at my concerts, hoot and holler
and tape the show.

I want her to meet her granddaughter,
sit in the front row
and tape her piano recitals.

I shout these things

in my car,
in the shower,
in my bed.

I want! I want! I want!

I tell my daughter,
"when I'm dying,
please feed me applesauce."

Openings and Closings

When my heart was ready,
I lifted my mother's album,
bulging and tattered from
so many openings and closings.

The binding, disintegrated
like her bones, the cover
a half-hinged door,
pendulous like her skin.

Glamorous headshots and movie stills
as Martha Graham's youngest dancer.
 Broadway programs,
New York Times reviews.

Square faded snapshots
with ombre scalloped edges,
long retired from their sticky
black mounting corners.

Here she is as a Thai princess
surrounded by courtiers,
her lissome hands doing
their own ballet.

Here she is as Dorothy
in toe shoes and a pinafore,
flanked by the Scarecrow
and the Tin Man.

A career of yellowed
clippings, faded photos
and a dancer
freed from their moorings.

I scoop up the flaky scraps
and watch as they pirouette
into her favorite vase,
next to the urn with her ashes.

Yahrzeit

One year ago,
a star, small and slight,
squeezed its presence
into my being, saying
"I live here now."

Nights, it whispers:
"Our tree is not severed
limb from trunk,
trunk from root,
root from soil.

In our dying,
we glow in our
children, waiting
until ready
to be passed."

Blue and Red

I
You
can't
get mad
at light blue,
placid lake and eye.
Red is another ball of wax—
all hopped up, itching for an argument or a fight.
Thank goodness for green, the great mediator, pointing out the pros
and cons of each side,
while yellow keeps whining, "can't we all just get along?"
Purple stumbles in high on weed,
orange does the twist.
Sometimes you
just need
light
blue.

II
I
like
red wine
better than
flowers because you
don't have to take care of red wine,
it takes care of you.
Please bring wine
next time
you
call.

Cool Reason with a Chaser of Tears
Found poem from letters by Lilli Tanzer,
1911-2004—painter, cartographer, Editor,
Haiku Society of America's Frogpond Magazine

From the day the seedling stirred to the power
of surge, strong enough to split a rock,
I have been seeing through a screen of my own—
cool reason flushed down with a chaser of tears.

I am seen as imagining, as part of my illness,
even the call of the wild turkeys.
Sixteen years of unspeakable hell,
invasion of my home and person,
voices since the beginning of time.

Tooth fillings can conduct radio signals.
The media slip these things in when they can.
All involved are to varying degrees, guilty.

Our bodies give us warnings—the jostling
of people and the rubbing against each other.
I must see to it that there is constant movement.
If permanent estrangement is to be avoided,
we have to be realistic.

When my own survival is involved,
I find it best to be tough, to be tender.
Our words and actions carry us to our
own punishments and crimes.
Do I choose being tough or do I compromise?
So far I have managed not to close any doors.

English in Freefall

Last Febuary, I was chomping at the bit to move, so I says to my friend, "If you don't mind me asking, do you have a realtor?" He was enamored with his, who supposably did do diligence, so I poured over her pamphlet and it peaked my interest. I contracted her and we conversated.

It's my perogative to live where I want, so I won't just make due. I proscribed my principle needs: large enough for my bedroom suit, a nearby library and an expresso or sherbert shop.

I waited with baited breath, as the idea of a peak at homes wet my appetite. I gave her free reign, and she preceded to comprise a list, appraising me of some track homes.

I was lost for words. I'm not adverse to the inter city, but I was taken back and went nuculer when I saw drug attics wrecking havoc on the sidewalks, a moratorium (who knows how many people are interned there) and a crumbling ampitheater. I began to loose my motivations when nothing passed the mustard.
I can attest it was a tortuous experience for the both of us.

We all ready seen allot when my inertia was farther nipped in the butt because by in large, her ideas were all together different than mine. She seemed disinterested in my prospective and for all intensive purposes, we just didn't jive.

When I inferred that I could of honed in on simular prospects myself, she was unphased, eluding to an admittance that she didn't mean to flout her expertness. But under her self-depreciating manner lurked a deep seeded intent to extract revenge and paint me as the escape goat. Irregardless, I use to be more sensitive, but now I'm just bemused. If she thinks I feel badly, she has another thing coming.

In this doggy dog world, affordable homes are first come, first serve. The media is in agreeance with the pundints who say that noone can afford to live here anymore. I told that mischevious realitor (tongue and cheek) that if worse comes to worse, I may have to adapt a different track, do a 360, and become an ex-patriot.

A Mobius Path

All hopped up between
wakefulness and sleep, I lose
myself. I dance 'round the Mobius
path, over the golden bridge, past
arching trees and skeletons doing
their own choreographed ballet.

I conjure up false memories,
engulfed in their dim party bulb
aura—our trip to London, my still
young mother with her long black
hair, the leafing tree that I stopped
watering every day but still grows.

Perched on a pinpoint in this
hypnagogic muddle, I don't get
around much anymore. I head
home on the wrong bus, forget
how to pee in the woods, forget
how to seek a landing strip.

So many openings, plump and sweet,
skipped. Rooted in good soil, they
do not leave gracefully; they wrinkle
and harden. As the film noir fog
descends in an unsettling gust, I
release its grip, look for openings
and hope to outpace closings.

Compelled to tell the world that I can
still do that dance, a tiny voice, someone
who loves me, whispers in my ear,
"Spring is the only season—
start another life."

GRATITUDE

Kim Addonizio for her invaluable workshops.
Kareem Tayyar for telling me I should do this.
Gretchen Marquette for her generous reading.
Interpoets for their extraordinary insights.
Ines. P. Rivera Prosdocimi for her expert help.
Nicole Roberts for her artistry on the front cover.
Jane Higgins and *Sandy Morris* for allowing me to use their artful photographs.
Ellen Seeling for being my rock.
Sha'ana Fineberg for being my other rock.
Harry Fineberg for supporting his daughters.
Mildred Fineberg for being my inspiration.
Eugenia Seeling for being my light.
Kitty Seelberg for sitting on my keyboard while I write.

Jean Fineberg is a professional jazz saxophonist, flutist and composer with an M.Ed. from Penn State University. A native New Yorker, she lives and works in the San Francisco Bay Area. Her poet father left a new poem of his on the table every morning, and Jean wrote her first book of poems when she was eight.

On the faculty of the California Jazz Conservatory, she has received multiple ASCAP music composition awards, an NEA Jazz Composition Fellowship, several Meet the Composer Grants, a composition grant from IntermusicSF, two grants from Chamber Music America, a Heritage Grant from the Doris Duke Foundation and nine music composition residency fellowships.

Jean studied with celebrated poet Kim Addonizio, and her poems have been published in *Modern Poets Magazine, Soliloquies Anthology, Vita Brevis, Dove Tails, Uppagus, Literary Yard, FLARE: The Flagler Review, Riza Press, High Shelf Press, The Fibonacci Review, The Creativity Webzine, Quillkeepers Press, Superpresent Magazine, Lucky Jefferson, Unlost Journal, The Jewish Literary Journal, Kerning, Jerry Jazz Musician, Parliament Literary Journal, Scarlet Leaf Review, Every Day Poems, Newtown Literary, Multiplicity Magazine, Workers Write!, Shot Glass Journal, Montana Mouthful and As Above So Below.*

She is currently at work on her next chapbook, tentatively titled *Memoirs of a Mean Sax.*

www.ingramcontent.com/pod-product-compliance
Lightning Source LLC
LaVergne TN
LVHW041505070426
835507LV00012B/1351